ANIMALS AND BIRDS OF THE BIBLE

ANIMALS AND BIRDS OF THE BIBLE

Willard S. Smith

Illustrations by
William Duncan

Abingdon Press

ANIMALS AND BIRDS OF THE BIBLE

Compilation Copyright © 1989 by Abingdon Press.
Adapted from *Animals, Birds, and Plants of the Bible* by Willard S. Smith, Copyright 1971 Church Art, Inc., published by Abingdon Press in 1974.

All rights reserved.
No part of this work may be reproduced or transmitted in any form or by any means, electronic or mechanical, including photocopying and recording, or by any information storage or retrieval system, except as may be expressly permitted by the 1976 Copyright Act or in writing from the publisher. Requests for permission should be addressed in writing to Abingdon Press, 201 Eighth Avenue South, Nashville, TN 37202.

ISBN 0-687-18298-0

MANUFACTURED BY THE PARTHENON PRESS AT
NASHVILLE, TENNESSEE, UNITED STATES OF AMERICA

FOREWORD

The Israelites were an agricultural people, familiar with the fauna and flora of both Palestine and Egypt. It is natural that the Bible should contain hundreds of references to animals and birds.

The ambiguity of certain Hebrew words in the original Scriptures makes accurate identification impossible in some cases. Then too, the early translators, ignorant of many animals and birds in the Holy Land, applied names of those they knew to the Hebrew descriptions. Thus they placed the badger and the ferret in Palestine, where they did not exist.

Research and modern knowledge have corrected many errors of the early translators. Certainly, this new knowledge should not change our love and reverence for the Bible. A better understanding of its words will bring a deeper understanding of its teaching.

The area that includes the lands of the Bible, often called "the crossroads of three continents," is the most populous skyway in the world. Nearly every kind of bird known in southern Europe, northern Africa, and western Asia has been seen in the area. Mentions of birds or allusions to them occur more than three hundred times in the Bible. For the most part, the bird watcher of that time saw the same varieties that nest in or migrate through the area today. Yet comparatively few are mentioned by name. Those described in the following pages are those that are named by the people of the Bible or would have been familiar to them.

Because of its universality, and keeping the above observations in mind, we have used the King James Version for references.

ANIMALS

A

ADDAX. Several kinds of antelope were known in ancient Israel. One of the most common was the addax. It is about the size of a donkey and off-white in color, except for its brown head. A short mane on the underside of the neck gives it the appearance of a large goat. It has a donkey-like tail, flat hooves to keep it from sinking into the desert sand, and unusual long, thin, double-twisted horns.

Like other antelope, the addax was acceptable under the dietary laws and so was widely hunted. It is so fast that no dog can catch it. Dogs are used, but falcons are usually a necessary part of the hunting team.

ADDAX

ADDER. See VIPER; SNAKE.

AGAMID. A large lizard, often three feet in length, covered with scales and thornlike protrusions, the agamid presents a very frightening appearance. Actually it is harmless, living mainly on insects.

The "tortoise" in Leviticus 11:29 is now generally thought to refer to some kind of lizard, quite possibly the agamid.

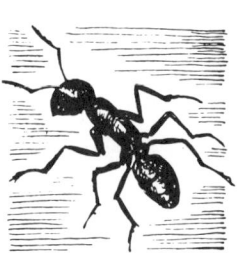

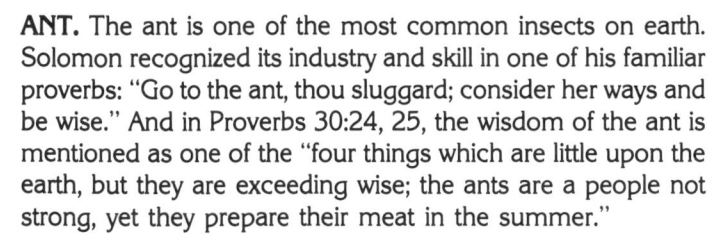

AGAMID

ANT. The ant is one of the most common insects on earth. Solomon recognized its industry and skill in one of his familiar proverbs: "Go to the ant, thou sluggard; consider her ways and be wise." And in Proverbs 30:24, 25, the wisdom of the ant is mentioned as one of the "four things which are little upon the earth, but they are exceeding wise; the ants are a people not strong, yet they prepare their meat in the summer."

ANT

AOUDAD. Also known as the barbary sheep, the aoudad was quite common in Palestine, especially on and near Mt. Sinai. Today it is found only in the mountains of North Africa. It has large, smooth, widespread horns and a liberal display of chin whiskers, which give it a resemblance to a large billy goat. It is related to the bighorn of the Rocky Mountains.

AOUDAD

APE

APE. The ape was not native to the Holy Land, but we read that the navy of Tharsish brought apes to King Solomon, along with "gold, silver, ivory and peacocks" on the long voyage from India and Ethiopia (I Kings 10:22).

Since the ape, along with other kinds of monkeys, was highly prized in Egypt, the Hebrews were familiar with it.

ASP. See VIPER; SNAKE.

ASP

ASS. The ass, mentioned more than 130 times in the Bible, was probably the most useful of all domestic animals. Because of its ability to thrive on a minimum of food, even a poor family might own an ass. It was used as a pack animal, for working in the fields, and for transportation. Yet it also was a measure of wealth. Pharaoh's gift to Abraham was many asses (Gen. 12:16). Job counted "five hundred she-asses" among his possessions (1:3) which later (42:12) had multiplied to "one thousand."

The ass of biblical times was a larger and more stately animal than the ass, or donkey, of today. It was usually tawny in color, the occasional white ass being greatly prized. Although once used in warfare, the horse superseded it in this capacity, and the ass became a symbol of peace. Thus it was most fitting that the Prince of Peace should enter Jerusalem that first Palm Sunday on a lowly ass.

ASS

AUROCH (urus). The huge auroch, or urus, was also known as the wild ox. Familiar to the Israelites, the animal was unknown to the translators of Hebrew Scriptures some fifteen hundred years later. The many references to the very large horns of the animal (Deut. 33:17; Ps. 22:21; Isa. 34:7, etc.) led these scholars to believe that the Hebrew writers referred to the unicorn. Hence "unicorn" in most references very likely should be *auroch.*

Probably the auroch is the only extinct animal to be "re-created." The last known auroch died in Poland more than three hundred years ago. Zoologists, knowing much about the animal, reconstructed it by what might be called reverse cross-breeding of cattle believed to be descendants of the auroch. Thus this huge animal of the far distant past—or a very close copy—lives again.

AUROCH

8

B

BABOON

BABOON. The baboon is not mentioned in the Bible, and, like the ape and other monkeys, it never lived in Palestine. Since it is quite likely that baboons were included in the exotic cargo brought to King Solomon's court from India and Africa, they may well have been known to the Hebrew people. Certainly the generations that lived in Egypt knew them, for the Egyptians looked upon the baboon with near reverence—sufficient reason for the Israelites to ignore the creature in their Scriptures. However, some scholars believe that "peacock" in I Kings 10:22 should be translated *baboon*.

BARBARY SHEEP. See AOUDAD.

BARBARY SHEEP

BADGER. See HYRAX.

BASILISK. This fabulous creature, half snake and half cock, was a product of a superstitious imagination. According to legend, the glance of the basilisk was sufficient to cause death. It was the symbol of the devil, a natural interpretation of Psalm 91:13, which, in the Douay version, reads, "Thou shalt tread upon the adder and the basilisk."

BASILISK

BAT. We know the bat to be a flying mammal, but it is not strange that the ancient writers thought of it as a bird and so included it with the stork, the heron, and the lapwing, as "unclean" fowl (Lev. 11:19).

There are more than a dozen species of bats in Palestine, living in caves and old buildings were they hang upside down through the day, flying out at night to frighten nervous humans, as is the case the world over. Isaiah, writing of "the day of the Lord," could think of nothing more degrading for the fate of the "idols of silver and gold" in "the last days" than that they be cast "to the moles and the bats" (Isa. 2:20).

BAT

9

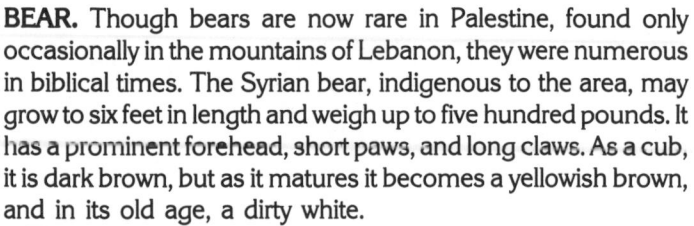

BEAR. Though bears are now rare in Palestine, found only occasionally in the mountains of Lebanon, they were numerous in biblical times. The Syrian bear, indigenous to the area, may grow to six feet in length and weigh up to five hundred pounds. It has a prominent forehead, short paws, and long claws. As a cub, it is dark brown, but as it matures it becomes a yellowish brown, and in its old age, a dirty white.

Though they rarely attack a person without provocation, they are extremely dangerous when aroused. Evidently Hushai knew this when he reminded Absalom that his father David and his followers, when enraged, were like "a bear robbed of her whelps" (II Sam. 17:8).

BEE. The bee is the smallest "domestic animal" in the world. Beekeeping was common in Egypt as far back as 4000 B.C. Honey was used for embalming, since it was the least expensive ingredient. And of course, its food value was well known. The Hebrews evidently took their knowledge of beekeeping with them when they left Egypt, since Ezekiel lists honey as one of the chief exports of Judah (27:17). Some of this might well have been wild honey, for wild honeybees were, and are, common in Palestine. But it is quite certain that Palestinian farmers kept domestic honeybees, selling both honey and beeswax.

Evidence that the potency of an attack of angry bees was well known is found in Deuteronomy 1:44 and in Psalm 118:12. In both references, the attack of enemies is likened to an attack by a swarm of bees.

BEHEMOTH. Job's mention and description of "behemoth" (40:15-24) has raised speculation among scholars as to just what animal he referred to. It was once thought that the ELEPHANT was meant. Now it is generally agreed that the description of its habitat, its great size and strength, its feeding and drinking habits best fit the HIPPOPOTAMUS.

The behemoth is the subject of many legends in Hebrew folklore, a mythical creature along with the unicorn and the cockatrice.

BOAR, WILD. Though once common in Palestine, the only mention of the wild boar in the Bible is in Psalm 80:13. It was a constant menace to farmers since a field of grain or a vineyard might be destroyed by wild boars in a single night. Since the boar is a pig, it was unclean by Mosaic law. Hence the farmer who killed the boars ravaging his crops could not use it for food.

It is interesting to note that in Albrecht Durer's painting *The Prodigal Son,* the SWINE with their tusks resemble wild boars rather than domesticated pigs.

BUBAL. The bubal, or Hartebeest, is one of several species of antelope found in parts of the Middle East. The Arabs call it a wild cow. In ancient times it lived in the arid regions of Egypt, probably as far as northern Arabia and southern Palestine.

Since the bubal seems to have been the only animal of the deer or the antelope family to survive in these arid regions, it may have been the source of the venison Esau brought to Isaac (Gen. 25:28). And the bubal would have been an important source of meat for the wandering children of Israel.

BUBAL

BULL. Since cattle were an important factor in Hebrew life, the bull was a practical necessity. While the Israelites did not deify the bull as did the Egyptians, with their bull-formed god Apis, and the Babylonians, who worshiped the winged bull-god, some of this obeisance found its way into Hebrew religious literature. A literal translation of "the Mighty One" (Gen. 49:24; Isa. 1:24) is "bull of Jacob" (Israel). Horns of the bull adorned the top of the altar in King Solomon's temple (I Kings 7:44), a practice condemned by later prophets.

BULL

BUTTERFLY. While butterflies are not specifically mentioned in the Bible, it is quite possible and even probable that in some instances the ancient writer had butterflies in mind when "moths" are mentioned. Certainly they must have been common. One can easily imagine the boy Jesus chasing butterflies in the fields around Nazareth on a summer day, the gossamer beauty of these frail creatures reminding him that the least of his Father's creations was a thing of enchanting beauty.

BUTTERFLY

C

CALF. Besides reference to the calf as a young cow, it is mentioned many times in the Bible in other connections. Probably the best known is the incident of the golden calf which Aaron had made for the children of Israel to worship (Exod. 32). Nor were the Hebrew people ever allowed to forget their

CALF

idolatrous transgression that so aroused the wrath of Moses. The golden calf is cited by the psalmist (Ps. 106:19); by the prophet Hosea (8:6); and in the New Testament by Stephen (Acts 6:39-41), in his eloquent speech just before his death.

A young calf was deemed an appropriate sin offering.

CAMEL. The camel is one of the first animals mentioned in the Bible. The fact that it could go for days without water and with little food; its ability to scent water before an oasis was sighted; its stamina and, when necessary, its speed—a camel can outrun a horse—made it of great importance to the Israelites. The species used was the single-humped dromedary.

Not only was the camel important as a means of transportation, but it was also much used as a work animal. Its milk, along with butter and cheese, were important items in the Hebrew diet. Cloth was made from its hair (Matt. 3:4), its hide was tanned for leather, and the dried dung was used as fuel and as an ingredient in roofing.

CAT. The cat is not mentioned in the Bible. The Israelites looked upon it with contempt. This may have been due to the fact that the Egyptians, their masters for generations, worshiped the cat; to kill one was a crime punishable by death. When a cat died, the Egyptians often embalmed it and buried it in an ornate coffin. Such pagan animal worship must have galled the Hebrews and made the cat despicable. And this attitude was probably hardened when their later captors, the Babylonians, kept cats in the sacred places of the temple. Yet in spite of this general feeling, it is quite probable that the cat was a household pet among Israelites of a later date.

CATERPILLAR. Since moths, grasshoppers, and butterflies were common in Palestine, caterpillars were familiar. They are mentioned many times in the Bible, often when pestilence is the theme (I Kings 8:37; Ps. 78:46; Isa. 33:4), giving the impression that the writers made no definite distinction between the wormlike larvae of insects found in refuse and the fuzzy innocent caterpillars of butterflies. But no doubt the Hebrews were aware of the wonder of the metamorphosis of the egg-larvae-flying insect cycle.

CENTAUR. Whether the people of the Bible knew of the centaur, we cannot be certain. It is quite likely they did believe in this mythical creature that has come down through the ages in imagination. It was supposed to have the head and torso of a man and the body of a horse. Symbolically, it represented man divided against himself, torn between good and evil.

CENTAUR

CHAMELEON. The chameleon was as familiar to the ancients as it is to people today. Its unique ability to change its color, not so much to match the background as a means of camouflage, but because of the temperature and its emotions, is well known. A most peculiar characteristic of the chameleon has to do with its eyes. Each eyeball can move independently, thus giving the weird effect of looking two ways at once—which actually it does! The chameleon is harmless, its diet consisting mostly of insects which it traps with a quick jab of its long tongue.

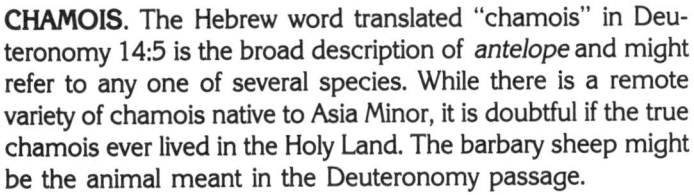

CHAMELEON

CHAMOIS. The Hebrew word translated "chamois" in Deuteronomy 14:5 is the broad description of *antelope* and might refer to any one of several species. While there is a remote variety of chamois native to Asia Minor, it is doubtful if the true chamois ever lived in the Holy Land. The barbary sheep might be the animal meant in the Deuteronomy passage.

CLAM. Since clams, along with other marine animals with no fins or scales, were classed as unclean in the Mosaic dietary ruling, they were not used as food by the Israelites. But they must have been known to the inhabitants of the seacoast towns.

CHAMOIS

COCKATRICE. It would do no good to look up the cockatrice in a nature book; like the basilisk, there never has been such an animal. Mention of it in several Bible passages of early translations (Isa. 11:8, 50:5; Jer. 8:17) was logical to the English translators, to whom the cockatrice—a kind of serpent hatched from a chicken egg—was a generally accepted creature, even though never seen. Later translators have changed this mythical animal into the very real "adder," as do footnotes in the King James passages.

CONEY. See HYRAX.

COCKATRICE

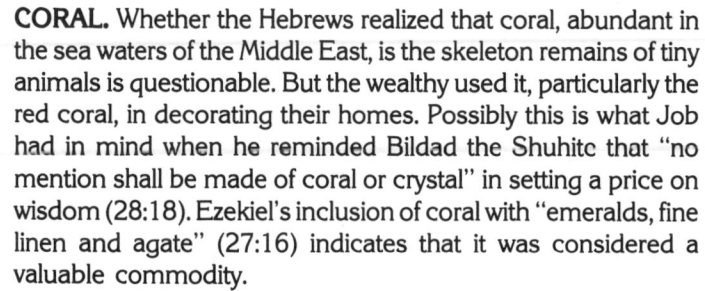

CORAL. Whether the Hebrews realized that coral, abundant in the sea waters of the Middle East, is the skeleton remains of tiny animals is questionable. But the wealthy used it, particularly the red coral, in decorating their homes. Possibly this is what Job had in mind when he reminded Bildad the Shuhite that "no mention shall be made of coral or crystal" in setting a price on wisdom (28:18). Ezekiel's inclusion of coral with "emeralds, fine linen and agate" (27:16) indicates that it was considered a valuable commodity.

CRICKET. Translation of the Hebrew word as "beetle" in the King James version of the Bible (Lev. 11:22) is changed to "cricket" in the Revised Standard Version, leaving us uncertain as to just what member of the grasshopper family was meant. In any case, we can be quite sure that the chirp of crickets, made by the cricket rubbing its hind legs together, was as familiar to the people of Bible times as it is today.

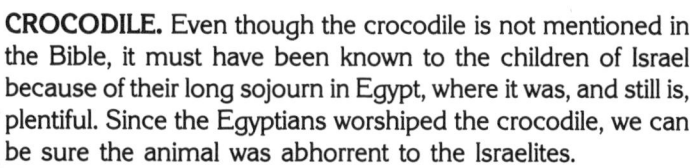

CROCODILE. Even though the crocodile is not mentioned in the Bible, it must have been known to the children of Israel because of their long sojourn in Egypt, where it was, and still is, plentiful. Since the Egyptians worshiped the crocodile, we can be sure the animal was abhorrent to the Israelites.

Some scholars believe that the crocodile once inhabited the Jordan River and the swamps of northern Israel.

D

DEER, FALLOW. The fallow deer, a small animal only about three feet high, lived only in northern Palestine. Some scholars believe a species of antelope was referred to in Deuteronomy 14:5, where the fallow deer is mentioned with the hart. This is not a repetition, as the hart is the male of the red deer.

DEER, RED. The red deer, a relative of the North American elk, was plentiful in the Holy Land. As mentioned above, the male is called a hart. "As the hart panteth after the water brooks" (Ps. 42:1) is a graphic word picture of a tired, thirsty male deer. The psalmist continues, "So panteth my soul after thee, O God."

DOG. To the Hebrews of biblical times, as to most eastern people except the Egyptians, the dog was an outcast, a scavenger to be despised. It is referred to more than forty times in the Bible. From Deuteronomy 23:18, where it is "an abomination," to Jesus' admonition, "Do not give that which is holy unto the dogs," this "abomination" is evident. The pariah dogs, belonging to no one, ran in packs, roaming and howling at night, subsisting on refuse and even ravaging human corpses. However, the Jews learned that dogs could be trained to warn of wild animals and thieves. Job speaks of "the dogs of my flock" (30:1). This could have been a type of shepherd dog somewhat similar to the ones we know today. But the dog was seldom a household pet. Even today, the worst of insults in Eastern countries is to call a person a dog.

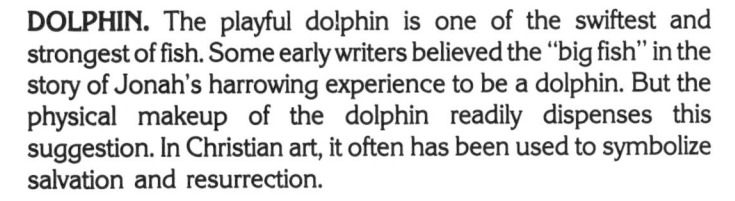

DOLPHIN. The playful dolphin is one of the swiftest and strongest of fish. Some early writers believed the "big fish" in the story of Jonah's harrowing experience to be a dolphin. But the physical makeup of the dolphin readily dispenses this suggestion. In Christian art, it often has been used to symbolize salvation and resurrection.

DONKEY. See ASS.

DRAGON. All ancient peoples believed in dragons. They are mentioned several times in the Bible, quite often as symbolic of evil forces, as in Psalm 91:13—"The young lion and the dragon shalt thou trample underfoot." Ezekiel could have been referring to the crocodiles of the Nile when he wrote of "the great dragons that lie in the midst of the rivers" (22:33). Just how the "real" dragons were pictured is difficult to say, but there was no doubt as to their sinister character.

DUGONG (sea cow). The dugong, a specie of sea cow, is found in the Indian Ocean and in the Red Sea. Hence it was known to the Hebrews. It is one of nature's strangest creatures—a mammal, as the alternate name implies, but lives mostly in the water like a seal, which it somewhat resembles. Its hide makes excellent leather of a bluish tinge and no doubt was used by the Israelites.

E

EEL. Eels were found in the local lakes of Palestine, and in the salt water of the Mediterranean. Since they have neither scales nor fins, their use as food was forbidden under the dietary law (Lev. 11:10). It is quite possible that *eel* instead of "serpent" was meant by Jesus when he asked, "If [his son] asks for a fish, will he give him a serpent?" (Matt. 7:10). An eel would be more familiar, and as worthless to a hungry Israelite as a stone.

ELEPHANT. Though there is no direct reference to the elephant in the Bible, ivory is mentioned often. A symbol of great wealth, it was one of the wonders of King Solomon's temple. Since the main source of ivory was the tusks of the elephant, the Hebrews must have known of this huge animal, even though they never saw one. It is interesting to note that the Hebrew word for ivory is almost the same as that in southern India and Ceylon.

The Asiatic elephant once lived much closer to the Mediterranean than it does today. When Egypt conquered Syria about 1460 B.C., a herd of war elephants was part of its army.

EWE. The female sheep was often a household pet of the Hebrews, as indicated in Nathan's story in II Samuel 12:1-6. It was seldom used for food or for sacrificial purposes, for the very practical reason that it was the mother of the next generation.

F

FISH. Plentiful as fish were in Bible times, and as often as they are referred to in both Old and New Testaments, no particular kind is named. But doubtless those caught by "the big fisherman," Simon, and his fellow fisherman were the same as those caught today in the Sea of Galilee and the fresh-water streams of the Holy Land. Familiar with fish and the vocation of fishermen, Jesus used them many times as illustrations in his preaching. One of his most challenging pronouncements was that his disciples should be "fishers of men."

The letters of the Greek word for fish, *ichtys,* are the first letters of the words of the Greek phrase, Jesus Christ, son of God, Savior. Hence the fish was one of the earliest symbols of Christianity.

FLEA

FLEA. The pestiferous flea was doubtless as much of a nuisance to the ancients as it is today. Certainly the unsanitary conditions in ancient times would have made it a common pest. The only direct reference to the flea in the Bible is by David, who chides Saul and successfully seeks to appease him by reminding the king that he is wasting his strength, seeking "a flea as one doth hunt a partridge in the mountains" (I Sam. 26:20).

FLY. Flies swarming over the land are listed as the fourth plague that ravished Egypt (Exod. 8:24). They are one of the most widely distributed of insects, as prevalent thousands of years ago as now, and of many varieties. The common housefly was a pest, but equally so were the botfly, or "gadfly," which deposits its eggs in the fur of a cow or other animal (Jer. 46:20). The tsetse fly, carrier of the germ of sleeping sickness, was familiar to the Hebrews in Egypt.

FLY

FOX. The Red fox was the most common in Bible lands, but the smaller Egyptian fox, rust-colored with a white belly, was prevalent in southern Palestine. The shiny golden Syrian fox was common in the northern forests. The fox always has been noted for its craftiness and cunning: Jesus referred to Herod as "that fox" (Luke 13:32). And rather pensively, he reminds his disciples that "foxes have holes . . . but the Son of Man hath not where to lay his head" (Matt. 8:20).

In the Song of Solomon (2:15) mention is made of "the little foxes that spoil the vines" of the vineyard. Foxes like the sweet juice of grapes and also burrow tunnels in the vineyards, which destroy the roots of the vines.

Samson's "300 foxes" (Judges 15:4) were more likely JACKALS.

FOX

FROG. Not only were frogs abhorrent to the early Israelites and "unclean," but the fact that their Egyptian masters paid obeisance to the frog-god Hequet made the creature even more despicable.

Frogs of many species were common in Egypt. The plague of frogs, second of the ten, is described in detail in Exodus 8:1-14. The psalmist reminds the children of Israel of this event in Psalms 78:45 and 105:34. The frog is mentioned only one other time in the Bible—in Revelation 16:13, when John tells of seeing "three unclean spirits like frogs."

FROG

G

GAZELLE. The gazelle is common in Palestine today. It is a member of the antelope family, especially noted for its graceful body and movements. It is one of the fastest of animals, leaping as much as three feet in the air as it runs. Very shy, it travels in herds of forty or fifty. It is hunted for food, but its speed makes special techniques necessary for the hunter. The animals are sometimes driven into narrow valleys where they can more easily be shot. Sometimes they are captured in nets, or driven into pitfalls. The Egyptians made pets of the gazelle.

GAZELLE

GECKO. The gecko has always been a common type of lizard in the Holy Land. The difficulty of the early translators is evident in the translation of the name in Leviticus 11:30, where listed among the unclean "creeping things" is the "ferret." But there have never been ferrets in Palestine. Later scholars concluded that the correct name was "gecko."

There is an old superstition that if a gecko walks on one's body, it causes leprosy. Even today many Arabs believe that it poisons all it touches. Actually it is harmless, though rather repulsive in appearance.

GECKO

GNAT. "Ye blind guides, which strain at a gnat and swallow a camel!" (Matt. 23:24). So Jesus, in strong hyperbole, indicates that he is familiar with the pestiferous gnat. It was a common practice to strain wine through cloth to remove insects and foreign matter. Hence Jesus' illustration was easily understood, effectively ridiculing the hypercritical legalism of the Pharisee's religious practices.

GNAT

While the King James Version lists "lice" as the third of the plagues to beset Egypt, all other translations list gnats. Perhaps there would be little choice!

GOAT. The goat of the Hebrews was probably the species with long, floppy ears, covered with long, black, silky hair. Both male and female had horns, but the male had an additional ornament of chin whiskers. It was an important domestic animal, providing meat, hair for weaving into cloth, hide for water bags, and even horns for trumpets. The skin was also used for the strings of the nebal, a large harp, and for drum heads.

GOAT

In addition to the above practical uses, the male goat was acceptable as a sin offering. On the Day of Atonement, one was chosen by chance, and after the high priest had symbolically transferred the sins of the people to the goat, it was turned loose in the wilderness (Lev. 16:20-22). We still refer to a "scapegoat" as one who bares the blame for others.

Goats and sheep grazed in the same pasture, but since the male goat was often ill-tempered toward the sheep, the flocks were kept separate. Hence Jesus' remarks in Matthew 25:32, "As a shepherd divideth his sheep from the goats."

GRASSHOPPER. Many varieties of grasshopper are found in the Holy Land, probably the same ones that were common in ancient times. The locust, as the most destructive, is mentioned most often. But the name also is applied to crickets and katydids, especially when the reference is to something other than the havoc wrought by herds of locusts.

GRASSHOPPER

H

HAMSTER. This small rodent is found in the Middle East, but is most common in Syria, where it is a source of food for Arabs. The Syrian hamster is somewhat smaller than the common pet, with a longer tail and silky hair of a golden color. It has large cheek pouches into which it stuffs food to be taken to its nest, burrowed into the ground. Each animal occupies its own quarters, consisting of a storage chamber and a "living room."

HAMSTER

HARE. The hare and its close relative, the rabbit, are common to practically all temperate regions of the world. Two varieties of the hare are found in Palestine. One lives in wooded inhabited areas; the other somewhat smaller species is found in the more barren regions.

Because of the ignorance of the times, the hare is classed as unclean "because he cheweth the cud" (Lev. 11:6). However, neither the hare nor the rabbit is a ruminant. But the peculiar way they move their lips—with which every child with a rabbit as a pet is familiar—does give the impression of cud chewing. On this presumption, it was classed as unclean and not to be eaten.

HART. As mentioned under DEER, the hart is the male of that species. It was used for food, and it might well have been a hart which Isaac bade Esau hunt, that he might have venison (Gen. 27:3ff).

HIND. The hind is the female of the red deer. Its use as food was forbidden. This was not for dietary reasons, but because the female was the bearer of the next generation.

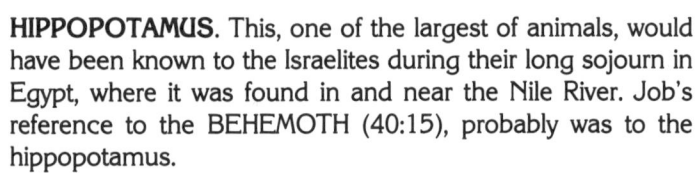

HIPPOPOTAMUS. This, one of the largest of animals, would have been known to the Israelites during their long sojourn in Egypt, where it was found in and near the Nile River. Job's reference to the BEHEMOTH (40:15), probably was to the hippopotamus.

The young are born under water and can swim before they walk. They weigh up to a ton when full grown. Job saw his huge creature as a demonstration of the creative power of God. Eaten by the Egyptians, the flesh was "unclean" to the Israelites.

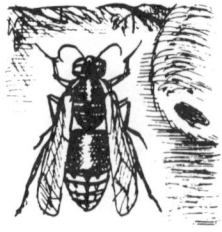

HORNET. There are at least four species of hornets in the Holy Land. The most common is the large yellow and reddish brown variety armed with the familiar poisonous sting of all hornets. Apparently they were as vicious in Bible times as today. Whether the promise of God to use hornets as one means of combating the enemies of Israel (Exod. 23:28) was meant literally or figuratively, its meaning is plain (Joshua 24:12).

HORSE. Though mentioned often in the Bible—more than 150 times—the horse never took the place of the lowly ass in the life of the Hebrews. Its use was mostly that of a war animal, vividly described by Job (39:19-25). First to draw chariots—Solomon had 1400 (I Kings 10:26)—but later as cavalry (Ezek. 38:15).

For a long time Mosaic law forbade the breeding of horses (Deut. 17:16) and they were imported from Egypt. But when the superiority of the horse in warfare became apparent, this law was conveniently overlooked. We do not know the breed of horses common in Palestine, but it was probably the rather small, swift animal common in Egypt. The larger Arabian horse was not known at that time.

HORSE

HYENA. The hyena was probably the most detested animal of the ancient world, due largely to its habit of digging up graves. Absalom was buried under a pile of stones to prevent this from happening (II Sam. 18:17). It was also the subject of many superstitions: its scent was believed to corrupt the air; sandals and leggings made of its hide were said to protect against hyena bites. Once plentiful in Palestine, the striped hyena is now rare. Strange as it seems, young hyenas are said to be easily tamed. Egyptians kept them as pets, and also as a source of food.

HYENA

HYRAX (coney). Probably the most familiar reference to the hyrax, or coney as it is more commonly known, is Psalm 104:8: "The high hills are a refuge for the wild goats and the rocks for the coneys." The translation, "badger" in the Revised Standard Version is misleading, since the badger is unknown in Palestine. The hyrax resembles a large rodent and is sometimes called a desert rat. It has a thick body covered with fine fur, short legs, a very short tail, and small, round ears. A marked peculiarity of the hyrax is the formation of its feet. There are skin folds between the toes. Glands on the bottom of the feet keep them moist and so provide a suction effect, most helpful to the animal as it climbs the sheer rocks among which it lives in colonies of up to fifty. It is a shy creature, its safety depending largely upon its ability to scamper into rock crevices on a warning signal from stationed "lookouts."

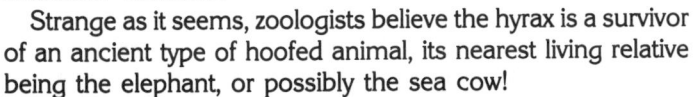

Strange as it seems, zoologists believe the hyrax is a survivor of an ancient type of hoofed animal, its nearest living relative being the elephant, or possibly the sea cow!

HYRAX

I

IBEX

IBEX. While the ibex is not mentioned by name in the Bible, most naturalists believe "wild goat" refers to this animal. Traveling in herds of eight or ten, it lived high in the craggy mountains, where sure-footedness and agility were essential. It is still found in Palestine.

When David and his followers were fleeing from the wrath of Saul, ibex may have been their main food supply "in the wilderness of En-gedi" (I Sam. 24:1). En-gedi was known as the "fountain of goats," quite possibly ibex.

J

JACKAL

JACKAL. A busy-tailed relative of the dog, the jackal is still common throughout the lands of the Bible. It was unknown to the English translators; "fox" was the nearest they could come to identifying the animal from the Hebrew description. It is very likely that the "300 foxes" which Samson caught, tied tail to tail, and turned loose as living firebrands to destroy the crops of the Philistines were jackals (Judges 15:4). Foxes travel alone, and capturing three hundred would be almost impossible. But jackals, traveling as they do in packs, make the capture of so large a number more plausible.

JELLYFISH

JELLYFISH. The jellyfish is found in the Mediterranean Sea and the Indian Ocean, and so would have been known to the Israelites living near the seacoast, but it is not mentioned in the Bible.

JERBOA

JERBOA. The jerboa is a rodent somewhat larger than the rat, common to much of the Middle East. Its hind legs are five or six times longer than the front, giving it a kangaroo look and, in fact, enabling it to leap like a small kangaroo so effectively that it can travel faster than a man. It has rabbit-like ears, large eyes, and is covered with a soft, sandy-colored fur, except for its white belly and a black and white tassel at the end of its tail. It feeds on plants and insects. It lives in burrows made in the hard, sandy soil and, being very shy, is seldom seen.

K

KERMES

KERMES. It is difficult to think of the kermes as an "animal" in any category. It is a nodelike insect about the size of a pea, found on the kermes oak. The dried bodies of the female, today as in ancient times, are treated with vinegar to make a scarlet dye that will not bleach or fade. This is the "scarlet" referred to in the Bible. Its permanence is what Isaiah refers to when he promises that "though your sins be as scarlet they shall be white as snow" (Isa. 1;18). This scarlet dye was very expensive and only the wealthy could afford garments of scarlet. Still, soldiers were often attired in scarlet, and it was a scarlet robe that the soldiers placed on Jesus (Matt. 27:28).

L

LEECH

LEECH. The leech (blood sucker) has not changed through the centuries. Its flat body is up to five inches long, with suction pads at each end. It has three knifelike projections in its mouth, with which it pierces the skin to suck the blood of its host. No doubt it was as repulsively familiar in Jesus' time as it is today. It is the only true worm mentioned in the Bible, where it is referred to as the "horseleach" (Prov. 30:15).

LEOPARD. The derivation of the English name *leopard* is interesting. When first discovered by early European travelers, to whom such an animal was unknown, they thought it a cross between a lion and a panther. So they combined the Latin word for each: *leo* (lion) and *pard* (panther).

The leopard was well known in Bible times, especially in the forested regions of Lebanon, where its swiftness and ferocity

LEOPARD

23

made it a constant menace to grazing flocks. It is one of the animals Isaiah mentions in his word picture of peace (Isa. 11:6). And Jeremiah indicates familiarity with the animal when he asks, "Can . . . the leopard change his spots?" (13:23).

LEVIATHAN. The ancient beliefs of the Hebrews in the field of nature coincided with those of other races in regard to strange and mythical creatures such as the UNICORN, the COCKATRICE—and the leviathan. While Job might have been describing a crocodile in Job 41, where the word "leviathan" is used, his people believed it to be a large sea monster, about which there were many fantastic legends. One such legend was that the leviathan was not capable of reproducing lest it crowded all other creatures out of the ocean! The psalmist pictures it as a playful animal (Ps. 104:26). In Isaiah 27:1, it is a serpent-like creature. Modern scholars are inclined to think that these and other references are to a mythical dragon.

LION. The lion, ensign of the tribe of Judah, is the most-mentioned wild animal in the Bible. It was probably the relatively small Persian lion, a species native to the Middle East. Though ferocious by nature and much feared, tamed lions were pets at the courts of the pharaohs, and later of King Solomon. Untamed, they also were kept in pits (dens). Into one of these "dens" Darius, king of Persia, cast Daniel.

The lion is used in the Bible as a symbol of strong spiritual qualities: "The righteous are as bold as a lion" (Prov. 28:1); as symbol for God (Isa. 31:4); and, by contrast, the devil is likened to a "roaring lion . . . seeking whom he may devour" (I Peter 5:8).

LIZARD. There are many kinds of lizards in the Holy Land. Unfortunately, the early writers of the Scriptures, and later the translators, were very ambiguous in their references. The sand lizard very likely was the "snail" mentioned in Leviticus 11:30 and Psalm 58:8, an example of the difficulty of establishing individual identity. Common in the area were the AGAMID, the CHAMELEON, the GECKO.

Less common than the other varieties was the land crocodile, some three feet in length, its body covered with green and yellow spots, with golden rings around its neck. The Nile monitor, common to Egypt, as its name implies, grows up to six feet in length. It, too, must have been known to the Hebrew people.

LOBSTER. The lobster is a marine animal and was eaten by the Egyptians and other maritime neighbors of the Israelites. But to them it was "unclean" and apparently they considered it of no importance. It is not mentioned in the Bible.

LOCUST. The locust, plague of the Middle East since earliest times, is a species of grasshopper. It is about two inches long, reddish brown and yellow, with a wing-spread of nearly five inches. In early or mid-summer, hordes of them, borne on the prevailing winds, begin a destructive migration. The result is as devastating today as it was when the plague of locusts visited Egypt (Exod. 10:13-15).

The Mosaic dietary law permits the eating of locusts. While the locusts which John the Baptist subsisted on in the wilderness (flavored with honey) could have been the insect, it is also possible that the reference (Matt. 3:4) is to the fruit of the carob tree.

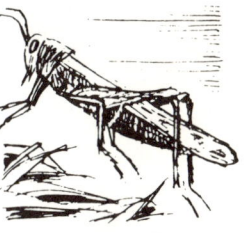

LOUSE. Human lice were as numerous among the ancients as among modern man where unsanitary conditions exist. Not only does the bite of the louse cause extreme itching, but the insect is the carrier of diseases, especially cholera and typhus. Human lice are of two kinds, head lice and body lice. Strangely, each stays pretty much in its own territory!

Plant lice of many species are older than civilization. The plague of lice was the third of the ten plagues to strike Egypt (Exod. 8:17).

LOBSTER

LOCUST

LOUSE

M

MAGGOT. The maggot, larva stage of the fly, is as well known as the fly itself. In most cases, biblical writers use "worm" in referring to maggots. "They shall lie down alike in the dust, and the worms shall cover them" (Job 21:26). Dead bodies are inferred here, which earthworms would not molest, but which soon would be covered with maggots. The loathsomeness of the maggot is manifested in the taunting challenge to the king of Babylon: "Thy pomp is brought down to the grave . . . the worm is spread under thee, and the worms cover thee" (Isa. 14:11).

MAGGOT

MOLE. The mole is listed among the unclean animals in Leviticus 11:30. And Isaiah (2:20) speaks of man's idols being cast "to the moles and the bats." Doubtless the mole was familiar to the Hebrew people, but "mole" might also mean the MOLE RAT.

MOLE

MOLE RAT. Though not mentioned in the Bible, the mole rat was and is common in Palestine. This leads us to believe that the word translated "mole" in some cases refers to the mole rat. It has much the same habits—burrowing into the ground, feeding on roots and bulbs. It has the same general shape as the mole, though it is much larger. It, too, has almost sightless eyes and is covered with soft, thick, gray fur.

MOLE RAT

MONKEY. Though not found anywhere in biblical lands, monkeys, particularly the baboon, which in Egypt was considered sacred to the god Thoth, were known to the Hebrew people because of their long sojourn in Egypt. As mentioned under APES, several species of primates brought from Africa and India were common in the court of King Solomon.

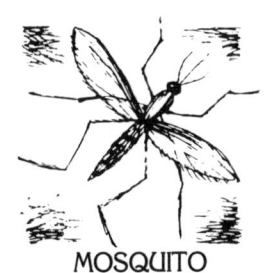

MONKEY

MOSQUITO. There is no doubt that the Hebrew people were acquainted with the pestiferous mosquito, including the Anopheles, carriers of malaria and yellow fever germs. The Hebrew word translated "mosquito" is not too clear, but we can be sure their buzzing and bites were well known. In fact, a kind of mosquito netting is mentioned in the Apocryphal book of Judith, where the author mentions one "with purple and gold and emeralds and precious stones" (Jth. 10:21).

MOSQUITO

MOTH. Probably the most familiar quotation concerning the moth is the admonition of Jesus: "Lay not up for yourselves treasures on earth where moth and rust corrupt" (Matt. 6:19). As every housewife who stores winter clothing in cedar chests and mothballs knows, it is the larvae of the clothes moth, not the adult, which does the damage. Evidently the ancients also had this problem. Job states it definitely when he cries out bitterly, "He, as a rotten thing, consumeth, as a garment that is moth eaten" (13:28). There were other kinds of moths, but only the clothes moth is mentioned in the Bible.

MOTH

MOUSE. There are more than twenty varieties of mice in the Holy Land. The Hebrew word *akbar* is used, which was a generic term applying to all species. The Mosaic prohibition against their use as food indicates that the people were familiar with them (Lev. 11:29). Prominence that seems out of proportion to their size is given the mouse in I Samuel. As a guilt offering for their theft of the ark (which they later decided to return), the Philistines were instructed to bring to the Israelites "five golden mice" (I Sam. 6:4), representing the five Philistine lords.

MOUSE

MULE. The mule is mentioned twenty-two times in the Bible, but only in the Old Testament, and only once before King David bade Solomon ride to him on a mule. The breeding of mules—a male donkey mated with a female horse, resulting in an always sterile offspring—was forbidden by Mosaic law (Lev. 19:19) But mules became so important to the Israelites that this law was often disregarded. Mules, combining the size and strength of the HORSE with the surefootedness of the ASS, became popular as a war animal, as a beast of burden, and as a riding animal for royalty (I Kings 1:33; II Sam. 13:29).

MULE

N

NILE MONITOR. Familiar to the children of Israel sojourning in Egypt, the Nile monitor is a large sand-colored lizard up to five or six feet in length. Its diet consists largely of smaller lizards, small birds, even tortoises and baby crocodiles, which also abound in the Nile.

NILE MONITOR

O

ORYX. The oryx is a species of antelope, distinguished by its extremely long horns. Most common in Arabia, it was also found in the Holy Land. Isaiah's animal translated "wild bull" in Isaiah 51:20 might well have referred to the oryx.

ORYX

OX. The ox, a castrated bull, was an important domestic animal, even in prebiblical times. It was used for plowing, as a draft animal, and was turned loose on the threshing floor, where its constant movement trampled the kernels of grain from the sheath. Jesus was familiar with oxen and must have made many an ox yoke in the carpenter shop at Nazareth. The yokes differed little from those used on the oxen of American pioneers. So familiar and important were oxen that Jesus used them as the excuse of the guest who refused an invitation to the banquet: "I have five yoke of oxen and I go to prove them" (Luke 14:19).

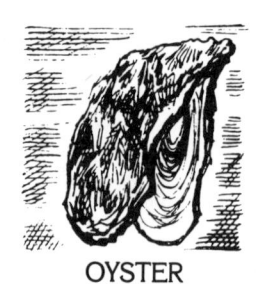

OX

OYSTER. Though the Jews were forbidden to eat oysters, they were familiar with this mollusk because of the pearls found in certain species, plentiful in the adjacent Red Sea and Indian Ocean. Jesus recognized the value of the pearl and used it as an apt symbol of the kingdom of heaven in the story of the merchant, who, when he found one pearl "of great price, went and sold all that he had, and bought it" (Matt. 13:46).

OYSTER

P

PORCUPINE. This comparatively small insect-eating animal was as familiar to the people of Bible days as it is today. It was often found in ruins and in deserted habitations. Curled up into a protective ball, its spines were ample protection against roving dogs or inquisitive men. The porcupine does not "throw" its spines, a mistaken notion held by many people. But they are easily pulled out and their barbed ends make removal a painful process.

PORCUPINE

R

RAM. A young ram was often used as a sacrificial animal, especially at the feast of the Passover. It very likely was of the broadtail species of SHEEP. The horns of the ram were used as

RAM

trumpets in battle. We read (Joshua 6:4, 5) that "seven priests bearing trumpets of rams' horns" marched around the walls of Jericho. Its walls crumbled on the seventh day, after a "long blast." Rams' horns were used also to hold liquids, such as oil for anointing (I Sam. 16:1).

RAT. No doubt the rat was as common, and as abhorred, in biblical times as it is today. The word *rat* does not appear in the Bible, but the word *akbar* included all rodents, rats among them. The unsanitary conditions of the times must have made its obnoxious presence inevitable.

The sand rat, native to Egypt and eaten by the Arabs, is the VOLE.

RAT

S

SCORPION. The scorpion has been called a living fossil, since it is a survivor of the age of the dinosaur. From the many references, Deuteronomy 8:15 to Revelations 9:3,10, the scorpion evidently was well known. The most common species in Palestine is the rock scorpion. Its body, from five to seven inches long, is made up of eight segments; the last five form a tail, at the end of which is its poisonous stinger. It has eight eyes and four pairs of legs. The pincers in the upper and lower jaws are used to hold its prey while the poison of its sting gradually paralyzes its victim. It lays eggs, which hatch in a very short time, the young living on the mother's back.

"If a son . . . shall ask for an egg, will [his father] offer him a scorpion?" (Luke 11:12) is a vivid contrast!

SCORPION

SHARK. Sharks always have been found in the Mediterranean and were familiar to the coastal inhabitants of the Holy Land. Strictly speaking, the shark is not a true fish. It is a selachian, the species of marine life which includes dogfish and rays.

The "great fish" in the story of Jonah's adventure could have been a shark. The great white shark is capable of swallowing a man, a feat hard to imagine of the whale, with its small gullet.

SHARK

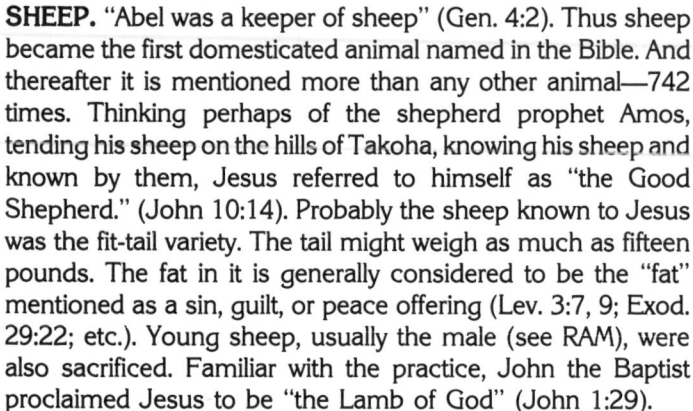

SHEEP. "Abel was a keeper of sheep" (Gen. 4:2). Thus sheep became the first domesticated animal named in the Bible. And thereafter it is mentioned more than any other animal—742 times. Thinking perhaps of the shepherd prophet Amos, tending his sheep on the hills of Takoha, knowing his sheep and known by them, Jesus referred to himself as "the Good Shepherd." (John 10:14). Probably the sheep known to Jesus was the fit-tail variety. The tail might weigh as much as fifteen pounds. The fat in it is generally considered to be the "fat" mentioned as a sin, guilt, or peace offering (Lev. 3:7, 9; Exod. 29:22; etc.). Young sheep, usually the male (see RAM), were also sacrificed. Familiar with the practice, John the Baptist proclaimed Jesus to be "the Lamb of God" (John 1:29).

SHRIMP. Well known to the Hebrews along the coastal area, this delicious sea creature was forbidden as food. Without fins or scales, the Mosaic dietary law classed it as "unclean."

SNAIL. Snails of many varieties are common throughout the Middle East. Yet outside the mention of it among the "unclean" animals (Lev. 11:30), the only reference is in Psalm 58:8. There the writer speaks of the "snail that melteth away." Among the ancients, it was believed that the slimy track left by a crawling snail was substance from its body, which in time would be wasted away.

The small marine snail was the source of the important "purple" (actually nearer crimson) dye that colored the robes of Assyrian, Phoenician, and Egyptian royalty as early as 1500 B.C.

SNAKE. From the time of Eve's temptation (Gen. 3:1), the serpent, as the snake is usually called in the Bible, has been a common symbol of evil. The horned viper, or "adder," of the Egyptian and Arabian deserts is mentioned five times. The reference in Psalm 91:13—"Thou shalt tread upon the young lion and the adder"—is familiar to every church school pupil. The bite of the adder is extremely poisonous. So, too, is that of the asp. Harmless snakes are plentiful throughout the lands of the Bible.

The ancients believed that snakes were immortal, that with each shedding of the skin, life was renewed.

SPIDER. The often obnoxious spider is named in Isaiah 30:28 as one of the "four things which are little upon the earth, but . . . are exceeding wise." And one must marvel at the "wisdom" of the spider, whose web, a trap for insects upon which the spider feeds, is woven according to a definite pattern of its own species. Even the first small web of the newborn spider is an exact miniature of that spun by its parents. The web, a liquid exuded by the spider, hardens on contact with the air and is placed in position by the insect's legs—"the spider taketh hold with her hands" is the way it is expressed in Proverbs 30:28.

Not all spiders are weavers, but most kinds construct some kind of web. A few varieties are poisonous.

SPONGE. We are apt to forget that sponges belong to the animal kingdom, though they are lowest form of multicelled creatures. There are many varieties, and since they abound in the waters of the Mediterranean Sea, the ancient Hebrews doubtless used them much as we do today. The mention of the sponge soaked with vinegar and pressed to the lips of Jesus on the cross is referred to in Matthew, Mark, and John.

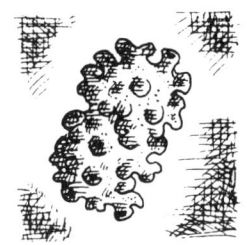

SWINE. Of all the "unclean" animals, the pig seems to have been singled out as the most loathsome. Even the swineherd, tending the pigs, was looked upon with contempt and was barred from the temple. The prodigal son (Luke 15:11ff.) sank as low as he could when he tended swine. It was so despised that the strictest Jews would not even mention the name. And they believed they would be polluted if touched by a pig's bristles.

As with the majority of other injunctions against eating certain flesh, the dietary law of the Hebrews was wise. The swine of ancient times were scavengers, their flesh susceptible to organisms that caused various diseases, not the least of which was trichinosis, which we guard against today. Moslems also are forbidden to eat pork, no doubt for the same reason.

One might wonder why there was a herd of swine into which Jesus could drive the unclean spirit (Matt. 8:32; Mark 5:13; Luke 8:33), since Jews were forbidden to raise them. This episode took place in the land of the Gerasenes, a non-Jewish community. The Gerasenes kept and ate swine, as did the Egyptians and the Romans.

U

UNICORN. The unicorn, a mythical creature of medieval legend, was said to have the head and body of a horse, the hind legs of an antelope, the tail of a lion, the beard of a goat, and a single, long, sharp, twisted horn. Actually, this imaginary animal had no relation to the animal the writers of the Bible had in mind. But the English translators of the Jewish Scriptures, uncertain just what animal was intended in some instances (Num. 23:22; Job 39:9; Ps. 92:10, etc.), called it a unicorn. Later translations have substituted "wild ox" as the likely subject.

URUS. See AUROCH.

V

VIPER. Many kinds of vipers are common to the Holy Land, and to much of Europe and Asia. All are poisonous, though some are deadlier than others. "The viper's tongue shall slay him" was the way Job expressed the deadly bite of a viper. Some scholars believe it was the asp Cleopatra permitted to bite her, causing her death.

VOLE. Water voles, also called water rats are found in Europe and much of Asia. The plague of "mice" that beset the Philistines as punishment for the theft of the Ark of the Covenant (I Sam. 6:5) might have been voles. The vole resembles a small muskrat with a short nose and small ears; it is dark brown in color and about six inches long, with a four-inch tail. It builds an underground system of passages, usually near water, hence its name. It feeds on plant roots underground, thus destroying the plant or tree.

W

WEASEL. Though mentioned by name only in Leviticus 11:29 among the "unclean" animals, the weasel was probably common in the Holy Land. The name of the prophetess consulted by King Josiah when Helkiak found the Book of the Law (I Kings 22:14; II Chron. 34:22) was "Huldah," a name which definitely means *weasel.* So the Hebrews were familiar with the animal.

WEASEL

WHALE. The humpback, the fin whale, and their near relative the dolphin, are found in the Mediterranean Sea. The Hebrew people living along the seacoast no doubt knew of them, even if seldom seen. The most familiar of the three or four references to the whale in the Bible is the story of Jonah "in the whale's belly." But as mentioned under SHARKS, the words "a great fish" is the expression used in Jonah 1:17. The Hebrew word translated "whale" is translated also as "monster" and "dragon."

WHALE

WILDCAT. Although the wildcat is not mentioned by name in the Bible, it always has been quite common in the Holy Land. It measures about two feet to the tip of its bushy tail, stands about two feet high at the shoulders, and may weigh up to fifteen pounds. Its fur is gray with a black stripe down the middle of the back and across the flanks. Though it occasionally attacks young calves, its main fare is birds, mice, and other small animals.

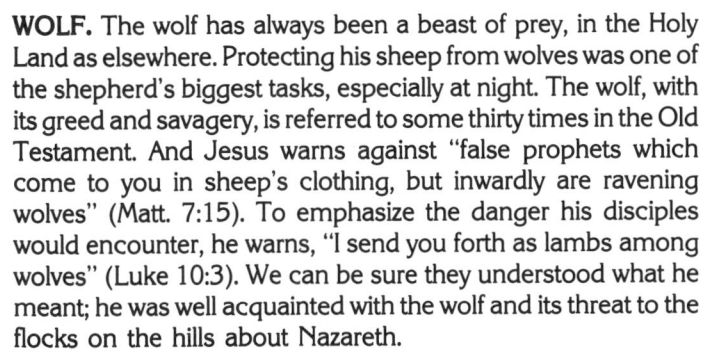

WILDCAT

WOLF. The wolf has always been a beast of prey, in the Holy Land as elsewhere. Protecting his sheep from wolves was one of the shepherd's biggest tasks, especially at night. The wolf, with its greed and savagery, is referred to some thirty times in the Old Testament. And Jesus warns against "false prophets which come to you in sheep's clothing, but inwardly are ravening wolves" (Matt. 7:15). To emphasize the danger his disciples would encounter, he warns, "I send you forth as lambs among wolves" (Luke 10:3). We can be sure they understood what he meant; he was well acquainted with the wolf and its threat to the flocks on the hills about Nazareth.

WOLF

WORM. The worm is mentioned many times in the Bible, although almost always the reference is to the MAGGOT or the CATERPILLAR. In an occasional instance, as in Micah 7:17, earthworms are obviously meant: "They . . . shall move out of their holes like worms of the earth." Earthworms have been common everywhere since the world was young.

WORM

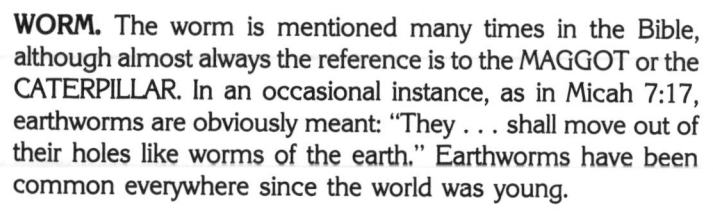

Z

ZEBU. It is quite possible that the "majesty" (Deut. 33:17) and the "beauty" (Jer. 46:20), rather strangely applied to the ox, were intended for the zebu, which it resembles in some respects. The Zebu is known as the East Indian ox, a much more majestic and noble-looking animal than the common ox. With its arched hump, massive shoulders, and short horns, it was known to the early Persians, Egyptians, and Babylonians. A close replica of the zebu is the brahma, now common in parts of this country.

ZEBU

BIRDS

B

BEE EATER

BEE EATER. The bee eater, or bee catcher as it is sometimes called, is aptly named, since its preferred diet is bees. It is a close relative of the kingfisher, though somewhat smaller. Of several species, the most common is gaily colored, with feathers of green, blue, and brown. An unusual characteristic, and one which makes the bee eater easily identifiable, are the two feathers which project noticeably from the middle of the tail.

BITTERN

BITTERN. A shy, solitary bird and a night prowler, the bittern lives in swampy places, where its brown and black mottled and striped back provides excellent camouflage. Unlike most birds of the heron family, its neck is short, nor has it the long wading legs of the heron. The unusually powerful call of the male bittern can be heard a mile away.

Reference to the bittern in Isaiah (14:23) and in Zephaniah (2:14) imply that Babylon and Nineveh were to become as desolate as the swamps in which the bittern lives and sounds its eerie cry.

BLACKBIRD

BLACKBIRD. The blackbird of the Holy Land is a different bird from our well-known variety. It is more brown than black and belongs to the thrush family.

BULBUL. The Hebrews discovered that the bulbul was an easy bird to tame and had a pleasing song. They kept them in cages outside the doors of their homes, much as we keep canaries today. The bulbul is rather a handsome bird, with shiny black feathers. White around the eyes gives it the appearance of wearing spectacles.

BULBUL

C

CHICKEN. The chicken is a descendant of the red jungle fowl of southern and southwestern Asia. It was domesticated long before the time of the Jewish settlement in the Holy Land. Though the Talmud forbade them to keep chickens, probably for sanitary reasons, lest the flesh of sacrificial animals be contaminated by the insects and larvae that breed in chicken droppings, the regulation was not strictly observed. This is indicated by the familiar words of Jesus: "How often would I have gathered thy children together, even as a hen gathereth her chickens under her wings, and ye would not!" (Matt. 23:34; Luke 13:34).

COCK. When "cock" is mentioned, there comes to mind the picture of the cringing Peter denying his Lord "before the cock crows thrice" (Matt. 26:34). Most often, the cock is mentioned in reference to its habit of crowing an hour or two before dawn. The "cock-crow" was the third watch. Jesus refers to this in Mark 13:35: "Watch ye therefore: for ye know not when the master of the house cometh, at even, or at midnight, or at the cockcrowing, or in the morning." No doubt the crowing of a rooster was the alarm clock of the Israelite farmer then, even as today!

CORMORANT. Common to Asian warm countries, the cormorant has two interesting characteristics: Though it has webbed feet it often perches on tree branches, and it swims beneath the surface of the water in pursuit of fish. It is nearly three feet long, covered with shiny black feathers. Its habit of diving in deep water where it fishes has given it the nickname of Plunger. Today Oriental fishermen train the cormorant to dive and retrieve fish. A ring is first placed around the bird's neck to prevent it from swallowing its catch.

CRANE. The crane referred to in Jeremiah 8:7 and again in Isaiah 38:14—"like a crane did I chatter"—was the European variety. The references to its "chatter" was an understatement,

36

perhaps in the translation, as all cranes have powerful voices. They live mostly in swampy areas, subsisting mainly on snakes, insects, and small rodents, a fact that makes them useful to the natives and probably fostered the belief that it is considered bad luck to kill a crane. All varieties have long legs and necks.

CROSSBILL

CROSSBILL. The crossbill is a finch. It lives among evergreens, feeding mostly on conifer seed, its crossed bill being especially adapted for extracting the seed from the cone. It is only about four inches in length. The male is a brick red, the female greenish gray. They very much resemble small parrots as they hang from a twig and reach for food.

CROW. While the raucous crow we know is not found in the Holy Land, the carrion crow of Eurasia and the hooded crow no doubt were known. Since these were quite common it may seem strange that the crow is not referred to in the Bible. One logical explanation could be that the crow belongs to the raven family and might have been intended in some places where "raven" is used.

CUCKOO. The cuckoo, spelled "cookow" in all but later translations of the Bible, was probably the European bird. Feeding mostly on insects, the fact that it does sometimes eat frogs, lizards, and small snakes made it "unclean" (Deut. 14:15; Lev. 11:16). It is a very clever imitator of other birds in calls and action. An unusual characteristic of the cuckoo is that some lay blue eggs, while others lay buff eggs with black spots. Oftentimes it will lay its eggs in the nest of another bird with eggs of a similar color, leaving them to be hatched by foster parents.

CROW

D

DOVE. The dove is probably the most familiar bird in the Bible, first mentioned when it was sent out by Noah and returned to the ark with an olive branch in its beak as evidence that it had found land (Gen. 8:11). There are many varieties of doves in the Holy Land, the rock dove, or PIGEON and the turtle dove the most common. They are monogamous, both male and female

CUCKOO

helping to build the nest, incubate the eggs, and care for the young. The newly hatched birds are nourished with pigeon's "milk," a substance secreted by the wall of the bird's stomach and regurgitated. Doves are characteristically gentle and often used as symbols of beauty and loveliness, as in the Song of Solomon.

All four Gospels speak of the Spirit of God descending "like a dove" when Jesus was baptized. Hence the dove has become the symbol of the third member of the Trinity.

DOVE

DUCK. Though not mentioned in the Bible, we can be sure that ducks were well known to the Israelites. Like the GOOSE they doubtless were served at King Solomon's banquets and in the humblest Hebrew home. There is no record that they were domesticated. Wild ducks are still plentiful in Palestine.

E

DUCK

EAGLE. Some species of eagle is found in almost every part of the world. The Holy Land is no exception. Of the three or four kinds found there, the golden eagle is probably the one most often referred to in the Bible. It is dark brown, the back of its neck tinged with gold feathers, hence its name. It has a wingspread of six feet or more.

The swiftness of the eagle's flight, its keen eyesight, and its longevity are used as illustrations throughout the Bible to illustrate a parable (Ezek. 17:3-10); to emphasize a situation (Deut. 29:49); to teach a lesson (Jer. 49:16). And there is something exalting in the declaration of Isaiah (40:31) that "they that wait upon the Lord . . . shall mount up with wings as eagles." In some instances Bible references to the "vulture" may have been translated "eagle." Both are of the same family and quite similar when airborne.

EAGLE

F

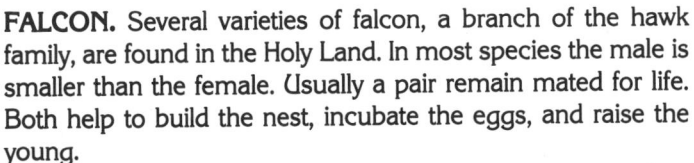

FALCON. Several varieties of falcon, a branch of the hawk family, are found in the Holy Land. In most species the male is smaller than the female. Usually a pair remain mated for life. Both help to build the nest, incubate the eggs, and raise the young.

The peregrine falcon has been used for hunting since ancient times; falconry was a common sport in medieval England, but there is no record that the Hebrews used them in this way.

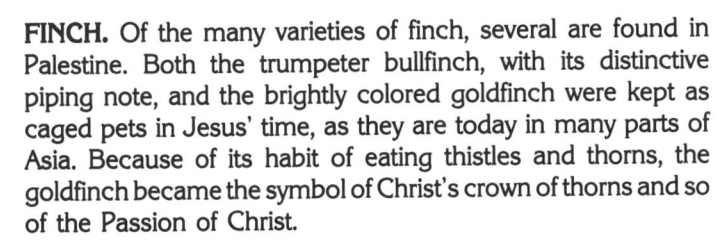

FALCON

FINCH. Of the many varieties of finch, several are found in Palestine. Both the trumpeter bullfinch, with its distinctive piping note, and the brightly colored goldfinch were kept as caged pets in Jesus' time, as they are today in many parts of Asia. Because of its habit of eating thistles and thorns, the goldfinch became the symbol of Christ's crown of thorns and so of the Passion of Christ.

FINCH

FLAMINGO. The long-legged long-necked flamingo was one of the many wading birds abundant in the Nile delta close to the site of the Israelites sojourn in Egypt. They must have been familiar to the Hebrews then, and later in Palestine when flocks of water birds, including the flamingo, inhabited the swamps around the Sea of Galilee.

FLAMINGO

FOWL. We think of a hen as a fowl, but "fowl" is used in a general sense to include all birds: God gave man "dominion over the fowl of the air" (Gen. 1:26). When Jesus bids his listeners to "behold the fowls of the air" that "neither toil nor spin" (Matt. 6:26) he obviously was not thinking of barnyard fowl.

FOWL

G

GOOSE

GOOSE. Though not mentioned by name in the Bible, carvings on the walls of ancient Egyptian tombs indicate that geese were known as early as 2500 B.C. The captive children of Israel surely knew them. It is quite likely that the "fatted fowl," part of Solomon's provisions for one day (I Kings 23:4) were geese, possibly the red-breasted goose, still seen in Egypt and in parts of the Holy Land.

GRIFFON

GRIFFON. A species of VULTURE, the griffon glides gracefully high in the air, swooping down to earth with amazing speed and precision when its keen eyesight locates a meal, usually a dead animal, far below. Then it may gorge itself until it is unable to fly. It is light brown, its neck and head nearly bare, covered only with fine down. The Egyptians and the Persians used the griffon as an emblem of royal power.

GULL

GULL. An occasional sea gull doubtless wandered inland as far as the Sea of Galilee, acquainting the natives with the bird. To those Israelites who lived near the coast of the Mediterranean Sea, and to Peter and the apostles who came to Joppa on the coast (Acts 9:36), soaring, screaming, sea gulls were a familiar sight.

H

HAWK

HAWK. Hawks of many kinds are common in the lands of the Bible. The most common in Palestine is the relatively small sparrow hawk. Job asks, "Doth the hawk fly by thy wisdom?" (Job 39:26). It builds its nest in the tops of tall trees or in rock crannies, from which its keen eyesight can detect a potential meal on the ground far below. Like all birds of prey, the hawk is "unclean."

HERON. The heron is characterized by its long legs, long neck, and long, pointed beak. The blue-gray heron is common in the Holy Land where it winters. It builds its nest in swamps and along river banks, often in a tall tree, returning to the same nest year after year. Quite often many nests are close together, forming a colony. Although some kinds of heron might be classed as "unclean" under the Mosaic dietary law, all are on the forbidden list.

The great white heron is found in the swamps of Syria. Common, too, is the black-crowned night heron, with a thicker beak and shorter legs than most of the heron family.

HERON

HOOPOE. The hoopoe is an attractive bird, especially with its crest of reddish feathers erect and expanded when it is alarmed. It is a fairly large bird, about ten inches long, salmon-pink, with zebra-like stripes on its back, wings, and tail. The nesting and feeding habits of the hoopoe do not match the attractive appearance of the bird. It does nothing to keep its nest in repair once it is built. During the incubation period, an oil gland at the base of the female's tail exudes an intensely unpleasant fluid to discourage would-be invaders. This, along with the fact that it has a habit of probing into filth for worms and insects gave the Hebrews sufficient reason for classing it as "unclean."

I

HOOPOE

IBIS. The ibis, sacred to Thoth, Egyptian god of learning, was common among the tall papyrus in which the baby Moses was hidden. Now it is seldom seen along the lower Nile. Over two feet from its slender arched bill to its tail feathers, with the long, thin legs of the wading birds, it was well known to the children of Israel before the Exodus.

IBIS

K

KESTREL. The kestrel is one of the smaller falcons and is still found in Palestine. Like all falcons, it is an excellent flyer, but a unique characteristic of the kestrel is its ability to hover in midair, its long, pointed wings extended. This has given it the name of wind hover. It feeds mostly on small rodents and insects. Kestrels are often seen in flocks of twenty or more.

KITE. A migratory bird, the kite summers along the Dead Sea and in the mountains of southern Judea. Like the falcon, it is a member of the hawk family. It is the greatest scavenger of the family, feeding on carrion, which assures it a place among the "unclean." But it is a magnificent bird, with a long forked tail and chestnut plumage. Like all hawks, its flight is graceful and buoyant.

L

LAMMERGIER. This is the OSSIFRAGE mentioned in Deuteronomy 14:12. It is a type of VULTURE, the largest of the species, with a wing spread of up to nine feet. It has been called the most magnificent of the birds of prey. Like most of the vulture family it nests on cliffs. It feeds largely on the marrow inside the bones that other vultures have picked clean. To get at the marrow, it carries the bones high in the air, then drops them on rocks to shatter the bone.

Because of the tassels of feathers that hang from its beak, it is sometimes called the bearded vulture.

LAPWING. The lapwing of Eurasia is a colorful bird, with dark-green iridescent feathers splashed with brown above and white below, and a black chest band. A curving chest decorates the back of the neck. About a foot long, it has stubby wings and the long legs typical of the plover family to which it belongs. But unlike the plover, it is not a shore bird and is usually found inland. Its eggs were once considered a real delicacy.

O

OSPREY. Spelled "ospray" in the Old Testament (Lev. 11:13; Deut. 14:12), this is a large fish hawk. Its head, neck, and under parts are white, the back and wings a dark brown with a blackish cast. Soaring high over the water, its keen eyes sight a fish, and with wings folded, it dives. It strikes the water feet first, often disappearing beneath the surface before it emerges with a fish clutched in its talons. Spreading its broad wings, it flies to enjoy its catch. Then it returns to fly low over the water to wash its feet.

OSSIFRAGE. See LAMMERGIER.

OSTRICH. The ostrich, up to eight feet in height, is the largest bird in the world. It once existed as far north as Syria and so was known to the early Hebrews. Job has much to say about the ostrich, none of it very complimentary (39:13-18). And it is true that the bird is not known for its intelligence—but it does **not** hide its head in the sand when danger threatens! It can run forty miles an hour and so can outrun most danger, but if forced to fight, it can deal terrific blows with its hoof-like toes. It cannot fly. Its cry, likened to the bellowing of a suffering bull, probably is what Micah had in mind when he speaks of "mourning like the ostriches" (1:8). "Owls" is used in the King James version, but ostriches are doubtless what the prophet meant.

OWL. In listing the unclean birds in Leviticus 11:17, the writer mentions "the little owl" and "the great owl." This is not strange, since there are many species of owls in the Holy Land. Very likely, "little owl" referred to the scoops owl, only about eight inches long. The large eagle owl might well be the "great owl," with a body up to two feet in length, strong claws, and cruel beak. Owls are nocturnal creatures, spending their daylight hours in ruins and caves (Isa. 13:21; Jer. 50:39).

The owl is the only bird with eyes that cannot be turned in their sockets. In order to see to either side, it must turn its head. Its sight and hearing are both very keen.

OSPREY

OSTRICH

OWL, EAGLE

OWL, SCOOPS

P

PARTRIDGE

PARTRIDGE. The partridge is widely distributed throughout the northern hemisphere. There are several kinds in the Holy Land. The most common is the chuker. It is covered with brightly colored feathers. The sand partridge is less colorful, its buff and brown plumage making it less conspicuous in the wilderness area of Judea. All varieties are hunted for food. Though a fast runner, it tires quickly. Hunters pursue it on horseback until the bird is exhausted, when it may be caught with the bare hands. Perhaps this is what David had in mind when he says that Saul came after him "as when one doth hunt a partridge in the mountains" (I Sam. 26:20).

PEACOCK

PEACOCK. The pomp and glitter of King Solomon's court was greatly enhanced by the gorgeous peacocks brought from India and the tropics by the navy of Hiram, king of Tyre (I Kings 10:22; II Chron. 9:21). They then spread to other countries in the Mediterranean areas.

The peacock, the male peafowl, with its gleaming colored breast and outspread tail of dazzling colors, has been called the most beautiful bird in the world. It became a symbol of immortality to the early Christians, probably because of the legendary belief that peacock flesh does not decay.

PELICAN. The pelican is one of the most curious looking birds. The long, flattened beak with a large pouch under the lower mandible, the small head, short legs, and massive body give it a somewhat ludicrous appearance as it awkwardly waddles along on land. But in the air it glides with grace on a wingspan of up to eight feet. Suddenly it dives straight down, landing with a splash and spearing the fish it has sighted.

The pelican's method of feeding its young is peculiar. The mother opens its beak wide, and the young pluck food from the mother's crop. This strange procedure led the ancients to believe that the pelican fed its young with its own blood. Thus the pelican became the symbol of mercy in ancient art, perhaps emphasized by the words of the psalmist: "I am like a pelican in the wilderness, seeking God's mercy (Ps. 122:6).

PELICAN

PHARAOH'S HEN. This is a small VULTURE, common in Egypt, as the name would imply. But it is also abundant on the plains of Sharon and the hills to the south, especially in the Kedron valley. It is white with black wings. Its large nest is built of sticks, rubbish, and even old rags. It wanders about the village streets, eating garbage and refuse that other vultures will not touch.

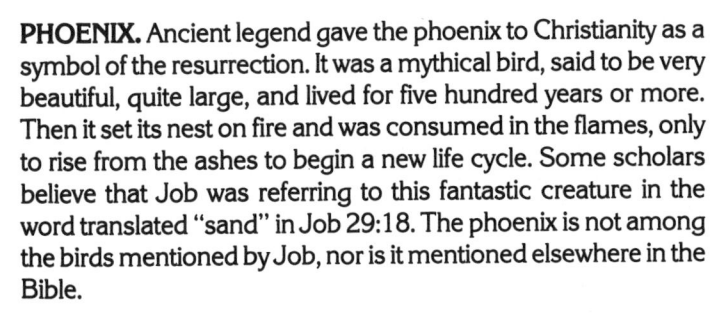

PHOENIX. Ancient legend gave the phoenix to Christianity as a symbol of the resurrection. It was a mythical bird, said to be very beautiful, quite large, and lived for five hundred years or more. Then it set its nest on fire and was consumed in the flames, only to rise from the ashes to begin a new life cycle. Some scholars believe that Job was referring to this fantastic creature in the word translated "sand" in Job 29:18. The phoenix is not among the birds mentioned by Job, nor is it mentioned elsewhere in the Bible.

PIGEON. The rock dove of Eurasia is closely related to the turtle DOVE, but it is a different branch of the family. It has been bred for five thousand years, and the breeding of pigeons is a popular hobby today. The ability of the homing pigeon to find its way back to its loft from a great distance is one of nature's so-far unfathomed mysteries.

Q

QUAIL. The quail mentioned in the Bible (Exod. 16:11-13; Num. 11:31, 32; Ps. 105:40, etc.) is not much larger than a robin. Its feathers are brown and black, except for those on the belly, which are white. Small as it is, the quail is still hunted for food, as it was long before the Hebrew migration to the Holy Land. The deluge of quail mentioned in Numbers 11—"two cubits high on the face of the earth"—no doubt is an exaggeration, but during the fall migration great numbers cloud the sky. Not a particularly good flyer, it covers the migratory route in short distances, settling on the ground overnight, often so exhausted it can be caught with *bare hands*, though nets are sometimes used.

PHARAOH'S HEN

PHOENIX

PIGEON

QUAIL

R

RAVEN

RAVEN. The raven is the first bird mentioned in the Bible: "At the end of forty days . . . Noah . . . sent forth a raven" (Gen. 8:7) to see if the waters had receded. Male and female, who pair for life, share in incubating and feeding the young birds. However, the raven's unsavory reputation is deserved. It attacks smaller, weaker creatures, often pecking out their eyes. They are predatory by nature, feeding on carrion.

In spite of their deserved reputation and uncouth habits, ravens are intelligent birds and can be trained to talk, parrot fashion. The raven with its "Nevermore" in Edgar Allen Poe's poem is not poetic fancy!

S

SPARROW

SPARROW. In picking a bird to represent the humblest of creatures, Jesus chose the sparrow: "Are not two sparrows sold for a farthing? And one of them shall not fall to the ground without your Father (knowing)" (Matt. 10:29). Sparrows are gregarious birds, flocks of them as common in Bible times as today. The psalmist might well have had this fact in mind when, alone and desolate, he wrote, "I am as a sparrow alone upon a house top" (Ps. 102:7). Though there are instances in the Old Testament where "sparrow" might mean any small bird, there is no doubt that many varieties were as familiar to the ancient Hebrews as to us.

STORK

STORK. One of man's favorite birds, the stock's purported association with human childbirth is common the world over. This may have come about because of the stork's loyalty to its young, both parents assisting in their incubation and care. The Hebrew word for *stork* means "kindly one" or "loyal one," both titles which one likes to think of as applying to human parents.

The stork is mute; it has no voice box. It communicates by rapidly clapping its bill or through movements of its head, neck, and beak. Feeding on frogs, fish, rodents, and lizards as well as insects, it is on the "unclean" list.

SWALLOW. The swift and graceful flight of the swallow as it darts through the air catching insects, was well known to the Israelites. Its habit of building its nest in barns, and even houses, might well have prompted the psalmist to write, "Yea, the sparrow hath found a house, and the swallow a nest for herself where she may lay her young, even thine altars, O Lord of Hosts" (Ps. 84:3).

The swallow, sometimes called martin, was very likely confused with the SWIFT by the early writers of the Bible. They are very similar in appearance, but not related.

SWALLOW

SWAN. Though the swan, common in Egypt, must have been known to the children of Israel, there is no mention of this graceful long-necked waterbird in the Bible, except in the list of "unclean" birds (Lev. 11:13, 18).

SWAN

SWIFT. Often confused with the SWALLOW because of its similar appearance and behavior, the swift is a member of the humming-bird family. It is probably the fastest of flyers, with much of its life spent in the air. Its legs are so short that its take-off from the ground is slow. When it alights for the night, it clings to a crack or crevice in a cliff, in position for immediate flight.

SWIFT

V

VULTURE. One of the most detested of scavengers, the vulture plays a most important part in nature's plan, feeding on and disposing of carrion (see GRIFFON; LAMMERGIER; PHARAOH'S HEN). This fact was well known to the israelites and in many places in the Old Testament, the vulture is plainly indicated by references to "fowls of the air" that eat dead flesh (I Kings 14:11; Psalm 79:2; Prov. 30:17, etc.).

VULTURE